REFLECTIONS
OF THE
Journey

A Mission
Trip Journal

With Commentary and

Questions by C. Delane Tew

New Hope Publishers
P. O. Box 12065
Birmingham, AL 35202-2065
www.newhopepubl.com

Cover design by Kathy Sealy

ISBN: 0-56309-540-8
N014114 · 0101 · 7.5M1

Dedication

*To My Parents,
Earl and Juanita Tew*

Introduction

Journey — travel or passage from one place to another

Journal — a record of experiences, ideas,
or reflections kept regularly for private use

You are beginning an exciting journey, a mission trip. Webster's matter-of-fact definition cannot begin to encompass the depth of meaning you will find along the way. Your journey will certainly involve travel, though. You may drive for four hours or fly for twelve, but when you arrive it will be a different place than the one you left behind. You will also be making a passage, but not just a physical one. You will learn many new things. You will change some attitudes about yourself and about others. You will bless others and you will be blessed.

Through each passage and journey of the body, mind, and spirit, take time to record your thoughts and your experiences. As an active, involved person you may feel hurried and lose track of thoughts you had during the day. God can speak to you through those thoughts if you will spend some time reflecting on them. This journal is a place for those reflections.

The journal is divided into three sections: **Before the Journey**—for the time before your trip begins, **During the Journey**—for during the mission experience, and **After the Journey**—for after the trip is over. In these sections you will find various subjects. Only the first subject in each section needs to be done in order. The others may be taken in any order you wish. Begin the journal at least one week before the trip and continue using it for one week after your return.

The subjects included will help direct your thoughts toward different aspects of the mission trip. Statements and questions throughout the journal may help you in putting your experiences down on paper.

Be honest as you record your thoughts and prayers. A journal is a private record. No one will look at it unless you choose to share it. Make the answers as long or as short as you feel is necessary. These questions are meant to spark your thinking and your dialogue with God. Feel free to let your thoughts flow from one question to other ideas that may be on your mind.

You may return to some of these questions on more than one day. An answer to a question from the first day may only become clear on the last day. Begin each day's entry with the date. This will help you see how your thoughts developed throughout the trip. There may be one question on a particular day that you want to spend more time answering. Do not feel like you have to write an entry for each question.

You will find that some questions overlap in the three sections of your journal. You may be surprised to find your thoughts on a particular issue changing over time. Be open to new ways of thinking as you participate in the whole mission trip experience.

Use the blank pages at the end of the journal for names of people you meet during your trip. This section can be used as a prayer list to help you pray for specific people with specific needs. You may also want to record addresses of some of the people you meet so you can keep in touch with them.

Make your journaling a time dedicated to God's work in your life. Include a favorite Bible verse that you think is relevant to the issue. God's Word is the lamp for our path and needs to be a part of our devotional time. At the end of each entry you may also want to write a brief prayer summarizing your thoughts.

Many people make journaling a part of their regular devotional time. Others set aside a separate time to write in their journal. You may choose whichever method best suits you. Remember, this journal is not meant to replace your regular daily devotional time. It is meant to enhance it.

PART ONE

Before the Journey

Your Team

When Jesus chose His twelve disciples, He brought together a group with varying personalities and gifts. The boldness of Peter was softened by the love of John. Matthew's openness to outsiders was coupled with Andrew's eagerness to bring his family to Jesus. For this mission trip you will be working with a diverse group of people.

Who are the members of my group?

Are there personality conflicts that may have
to be resolved within the group?

What special gifts and abilities does each one
bring to the group?

_____

_____

_____

_____

_____

_____

_____

_____

_____

_____

_____

_____

_____

_____

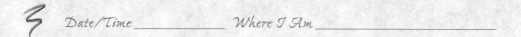

Home Alone

Leaving for a mission trip can be a traumatic experience. You are a responsible person with an active life. You may feel guilty about the work that will go undone while you are gone and about the loved ones you will leave behind.

*W*hat responsibilities am I asking someone else to handle?

*H*ow do I feel about turning these responsibilities over to them?

*H*ow do I know God will take care of things in my absence?

_____

_____

_____

_____

_____

_____

_____

_____

_____

_____

_____

_____

_____

_____

_____

_____

Special in God's Sight

You are a gifted and talented person, a special creation loved by God. All those little quirks that you sometimes wish you didn't have are part of the uniqueness of character that God had in mind for you from the beginning of time.

What are my special gifts and abilities?

How do I use these in my everyday life?

How might these be used during this mission trip?

_____
_____
_____
_____
_____
_____
_____
_____
_____
_____
_____
_____
_____
_____
_____
_____
_____

Sight Unseen

Arriving in a strange city, whether it is around the world or in a neighboring state, can be an unsettling experience. You can allay many of these fears by learning all you can about the place you will serve. Look for information in newspaper and magazine articles, in an encyclopedia, or on the Internet. These are just a few of the questions you may want to answer.

*W*hat will the weather be like?

*W*hat is the population of the area?

*W*hat is the main religion of the area?

_____
_____
_____
_____
_____
_____
_____
_____
_____
_____
_____
_____
_____
_____
_____
_____
_____
_____
_____
_____

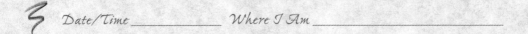

Plan for the Unplanned

On a mission field only one thing is certain—something unpredictable will happen. On this trip you will be faced with a multitude of variables: weather, local facilities, available resources, neighborhood reaction. If you expect everything to happen just as you have planned, you are bound to be disappointed. The most important attitude for mission volunteers to carry with them is *flexibility*. Think about your response to changing circumstances.

Am I open to changing my plans?

Is it easy for me to be flexible?

How can I be more flexible?

_____

_____

_____

_____

_____

_____

_____

_____

_____

_____

_____

_____

_____

_____

_____

_____

Assumptions

You have learned some things about the place where you will serve and the people to whom you will minister. Many times we form images in our minds about certain kinds of people. These assumptions can be an obstacle to ministry.

What assumptions have I made about the people I will serve?

How did I form these assumptions?

How does my attitude need to change?

_____

_____

_____

_____

_____

_____

_____

_____

_____

_____

_____

_____

_____

_____

_____

_____

_____

_____

The Greatest Story

During your time of ministry you will be sharing in various ways. Your laughter will brighten someone's dark day. A song you sing will soften a hard heart. You will share a Bible story with a child who has never heard about Moses or Daniel or Jesus. The greatest story that you have to share is your own testimony. You can be a living witness that God is alive in this world.

How did I become a Christian?

How have I changed since that day?

How does God make a difference in my life today?

_____

_____

_____

_____

_____

_____

_____

_____

_____

_____

_____

_____

_____

_____

_____

_____

_____

_____

_____

_____

_____

_____

Other Thoughts Before My Trip

PART TWO

During the Journey

Travel Day

This is the day! Your bags are packed. You've worked hard to prepare for this trip and now it's here. You may have great expectations for this experience. Sometimes our expectations can get us into trouble. If you are expecting a four-star hotel and you find yourself staying at a youth hostel with a bathroom on the hall, you may be disappointed with your whole mission trip. It is important to have a clear understanding of this trip and your purpose.

What are my expectations of this trip: travel plans, where I will stay, the ministry I will be conducting?

How might these expectations limit my ability to serve?

What is the main thing that will need to happen in order for me to call this mission trip a success?

How am I feeling physically and mentally as I begin this trip?

_____

_____

_____

_____

_____

_____

_____

_____

_____

_____

_____

_____

_____

_____

_____

_____

At the Starting Line

Ready-or-not, the work starts today. You have planned long and hard to get ready for today. Regardless of what kind of ministry you will be conducting, whether it is a Backyard Bible Club, a construction project, or a prayerwalking journey, you will be meeting people from the local area. They may be skeptical about your reasons for coming. They may laugh at your accent or your attempts at their language. These are the people to whom you will be ministering for the whole trip.

*W*hat kind of first impression do I want to make?

*W*hat will I need to do to make that impression?

*W*hen they ask me why I am here
what reason do I want to give them?

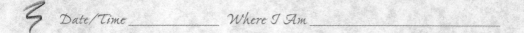

Recovery from Traveling

You have arrived. Usually traveling leaves a person a little worn out. Traveling can be a group-building time, but long plane or car rides can also wear on people's nerves.

$\mathcal{D}$id something happen on the trip that I would like
to remember, perhaps an experience that made everyone laugh?

$\mathcal{W}$as there a time when tempers flared
and unkind words were spoken?

$\mathcal{I}$s there anything I need to do to help the group
get over this event?

_____
_____
_____
_____
_____
_____
_____
_____
_____
_____
_____
_____
_____
_____
_____
_____
_____
_____
_____

Your Situation

Now that you are here and getting settled, describe what things have actually been like so far. Come back to this journal entry to describe changes that occur during your trip.

Where do I sleep?
Where do I work and minister during the day?
What am I doing during the day?
With whom do I work most closely?

_____

_____

_____

_____

_____

_____

_____

_____

_____

_____

_____

_____

_____

_____

_____

_____

_____

_____

Ministering to the Multitudes

You are well into your ministry now. You may be feeling like the disciples felt when Jesus told them to feed the 5,000. It is easy to be overwhelmed by the needs. Remember that effective ministry happens one-on-one.

*W*ho are some individuals I have met during my trip?

*W*hat are their needs?

*H*ow can I equip them to help themselves in the future?

*W*hat do they need from me to enable them to be more fully what God created them to be?

_____

_____

_____

_____

_____

_____

_____

_____

_____

_____

_____

_____

_____

_____

_____

_____

_____

_____

_____

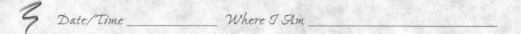

Breathing Room

Jesus reached out and touched thousands during His three years of public ministry. However, He also understood the need to stop what He was doing and get away from the crowds from time to time. You can give of yourself so much that you feel empty. Even on a short mission trip, you can quickly get to the breaking point.

How do I feel today physically?

What have been the greatest physical and mental strains for me?

Has my group scheduled personal quiet time and time for play and relaxation during the trip?

What can I do today that would help me get away and relax, even if only for a brief period of time?

_____

___

_____

_____

_____

_____

_____

_____

_____

_____

_____

_____

_____

_____

_____

_____

Teamwork

By now you have had a chance to see your team work in a wide variety of situations. Before you began the trip, you described your team members in this journal. Look back at that entry.

*D*o I see any of my team members in a different light now?

*W*hich team members are displaying gifts and abilities that I did not see before?

*W*hat new things have I discovered about myself during this trip?

_____

_____

_____

_____

_____

_____

_____

_____

_____

_____

_____

_____

_____

_____

_____

_____

_____

_____

_____

Cultural Differences

Traveling brings us into contact with different cultures. Suburbanites and inner-city dwellers look at life in completely different ways. Whether you have crossed the ocean or crossed the railroad tracks, you have been dealing with a new culture. Missionaries often share that they have gained a fuller understanding of who God is by looking at God through the eyes of another culture.

*W*hat cultural differences have I become aware of?

*H*ow do these differences make sharing God's love more difficult?

*H*ave I discovered something new about God during this trip?

_____

_____

_____

_____

_____

_____

_____

_____

_____

_____

_____

_____

_____

_____

_____

_____

_____

_____

_____

Mary and Martha

The story of these two sisters from the Bible is a familiar one. Martha spent her time concerned over the details of the day's needs. Mary spent her time worshiping at the feet of Jesus. Mission volunteers need to find a balance between these two needs. The need to take care of details is important. The need to worship is also important.

What are my responsibilities during this trip?

Are there any details that have been giving me trouble?

How can I worship God in the midst of my work today?

_____

_____

_____

_____

_____

_____

_____

_____

_____

_____

_____

_____

_____

_____

_____

_____

_____

_____

_____

_____

_____

A Gift of Grace

Today's news media are often filled with stories of violence, ignorance, and poverty walking hand in hand. It is easy, looking in from the outside, to become judgmental toward individuals who are trapped in this cycle. Coming face-to-face with the individuals who have lost hope that life can be better gives us a new perspective. We need to remember that we are all sinners saved by grace. Just as we have received grace from God, we need to give it to others.

*H*ave I found myself being judgmental toward some of the people I have met this week?

*W*hat made me feel judgmental?

*H*ow can I show God's grace today?

_____

_____

_____

_____

_____

_____

_____

_____

_____

_____

_____

_____

_____

_____

_____

_____

_____

_____

_____

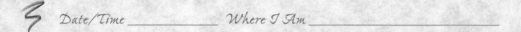

Image-Bearers

"The apple never falls far from the tree" is a phrase often used when comparing a child to a parent. As children of God we are to show the characteristics of God in this world. We are created in the image of God, each endowed with unique gifts and abilities. Through the power of the Holy Spirit we are to be godly image-bearers wherever we go. Genesis tells us that humankind was created in the image of God. That means that somewhere under the need, the hurt, the anger, and the sin of people you work with today lies the image of God.

How can I be a better image-bearer today?

How can I use the gifts I have to bless others during my ministry?

Can I see the image of God in the people around me?
(List some of the people you have gotten to know on this trip
and a characteristic of God you see in them.)

_____

_____

_____

_____

_____

_____

_____

_____

_____

_____

_____

_____

_____

_____

_____

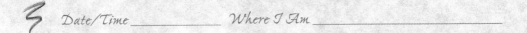

Failures and Faith

Even when we have the best intentions, things may not turn out the way we expect. We learn from events that don't go well and from our own trials and errors. Most importantly, we learn that God is faithful and is greater than the obstacles we see.

*W*hat plans haven't gone as expected?

*H*ave I been able to adapt or change something to make it more effective?

*H*ave I learned more effective ways to accomplish God's purposes based on these individuals and their circumstances?

_____

_____

_____

_____

_____

_____

_____

_____

_____

_____

_____

_____

_____

_____

_____

_____

_____

_____

_____

_____

_____

_____

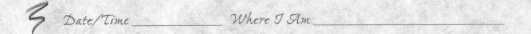

The Voice of God

If God would write His will for our lives across the sky, then we would be certain to know the best thing to do. God has not chosen to work that way. God speaks to us through various instruments—Holy Scripture, a sermon, a book, a life.

*H*ow have I heard God speaking to me this week?

*W*hat is God saying to me?

*H*ow will I obey?

_____

_____

_____

_____

_____

_____

_____

_____

_____

_____

_____

_____

_____

_____

_____

_____

_____

_____

_____

Other Thoughts During My Trip

PART THREE

After the Journey

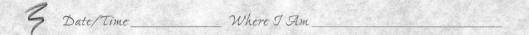

There's No Place Like Home

After a trip, it is important to take time and catch up with your friends and family who stayed behind. Unfortunately, all those responsibilities you left undone while you were gone will be vying for your time. Perhaps you will be rushing back to work or to school or to responsibilities at home.

How can I spend special time with those nearest to me?

What experiences from the trip do I want to share with them?

What can I do to say thank you to those who helped take care of things while I was away?

_____
_____
_____
_____
_____
_____
_____
_____
_____
_____
_____
_____
_____
_____
_____
_____
_____
_____

Bringing the Ministry Home

The skills you learned and the ministry you developed don't have to be left on your mission trip.

Where in my area would I find people with the same needs as those I met on my trip?

How can I find out if any ministry is being conducted in that area?

What would I need to do to be involved in ongoing ministry?

_____

_____

_____

_____

_____

_____

_____

_____

_____

_____

_____

_____

_____

_____

_____

_____

_____

_____

_____

_____

_____

Memories

Some special things happened on your trip. These are things you will want to remember. Writing about those events will help you remember them and will help you know how to share them with others.

*W*hat was the funniest thing that happened to me or to someone in the group?

*W*hat was the most meaningful event for me?

*W*hich person will I remember the most?

_____

_____

_____

_____

_____

_____

_____

_____

_____

_____

_____

_____

_____

_____

_____

_____

_____

_____

_____

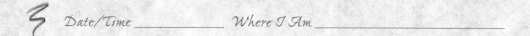

Going Separate Ways

It's amazing how spending every waking moment with a group of people can form you into something that resembles a family. You and the other members of your group shared a very significant event together.

What are some special things I saw my team do to help others?

What is one characteristic of each of my team members that I discovered on our trip?

How did I fit into the team?

_____

_____

_____

_____

_____

_____

_____

_____

_____

_____

_____

_____

_____

_____

_____

_____

_____

_____

_____

_____

God's Work

One special thing about going on a mission trip is that for one period of time you can give yourself totally to the work of God. You don't have to be distracted by the everyday cares that usually take up your time. You have a chance to give your all to an effort and then stand back and see God at work.

How did I see God at work during my trip?
How did God work through me?
How did I grow spiritually while I was doing the will of God?

Peoples Is Peoples

When asked what he thought of the people he had met on his first trip to the city, the country farmer replied, "Peoples is peoples." Your world vision was broadened during your mission trip. You learned new things about new people and new places. You also learned that no matter the cultural differences, all people everywhere need God's love.

What surprised me most about the situation in which I was working?

What surprised me most about the people with whom I worked?

What was the hardest part about working with the people?

_____

_____

_____

_____

_____

_____

_____

_____

_____

_____

_____

_____

_____

_____

_____

_____

_____

_____

Sharing with Your Church

Perhaps people in your church supported you financially or with prayer while you were on your trip. Maybe they commissioned you or had a special time of prayer for you. Whether or not your church was involved in your ministry, they should know what God is doing around the world and how they, too, can be a part of it.

*W*hat is the one thing I would like to share
with my church family about the trip?

*H*ow can I make it possible next year
for someone new to go on a mission trip?

_____
_____
_____
_____
_____
_____
_____
_____
_____
_____
_____
_____
_____
_____
_____
_____

Other Thoughts After My Trip